"An exquisite invitation for us all to enter the immense world of nature and discover a new level of beauty, majesty, power, intelligence, and wisdom. The combination of nature speaking to us through Kathleen Thormod Carr's photography and Dorothy Maclean's messages serves to beckon us to move forward and say 'Yes!' to developing our own working, cocreative partnership with nature."

—Machaelle Small Wright, author of *Behaving as If the God in All Life Mattered*

"A unique and powerful book! The external beauty of nature and its inner voice expressed through poetic vision merge in harmony to convey a lesson of vital importance."

—Stanislav Grof, author of *The Adventure of Self-Discovery*

"Beauty, harmony, and oneness with all life pour through the words and the photography in this beautiful book, *To Honor the Earth,* that Dorothy Maclean and Kathy Thormod Carr have created. Open your hearts and minds and feel it, see it, and be it; we are all part of Mother Earth."

—Eileen M. Caddy, cofounder of the Findhorn Community

"*To Honor the Earth* focuses on the most essential task for contemporary consciousness: the reappropriation of the forgotten and repressed elements of the primal mind. In the text and in the photography there lives that wonder of the universe, that felt majesty, and that depth of communion that was once common to humanity but has been lost to recent generations."

—Brian Swimme, author of *The Universe Is a Green Dragon*

"This book eloquently reminds us that we are not alone or lonely in our Earth-healing work. The voices of the Earth speak clearly through these pages—compelling, inviting, teaching us to reconnect. The voices of the trees are especially powerful in the urgency of their warnings of danger. The photographs are beautiful and uplifting."

  —John Seed, coauthor of *Thinking Like a Mountain,* editor of *World Rainforest Report*

"There are many ways to explore nature and discover its immense mysteries. Scientists dissect and decode nature with microscopes and computers, and the realms they have discovered are truly wonderful. There is another, lesser-known path to knowledge and association with the natural world. Dorothy Maclean is one of its clearest and most profound exponents. She attunes herself closely to the Earth and with its creatures, and they speak to, and through, her. Hers is a gentle shamanistic tradition in which communication with nature is direct, profound, and relevant to the fate of our species."

  —John Todd, Ph.D., president of Ocean Arks International and director of its Center for the Protection and Restoration of Waters

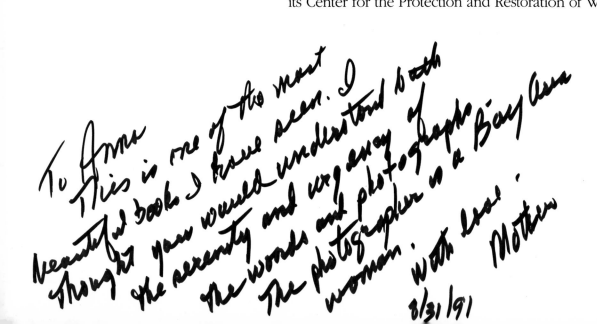

To Anne

This is one of the most beautiful books I have seen. I thought you would understand both the serenity and urgency of the words and photographs of The photographer is a Bay Area woman. With love!

Mother

8/31/91

To Honor the Earth

Other books by Dorothy Maclean and Kathleen Thormod Carr:

The Findhorn Garden, by the Findhorn Community

To Hear the Angels Sing, by Dorothy Maclean

Also available from HarperSanFrancisco:

2 Minutes a Day for a Greener Planet, by Marjorie Lamb

Mother Earth Spirituality: Native American Paths to Healing Ourselves and Our World,
by Ed McGaa (Eagle Man)

A Passion for This Earth: Exploring a New Partnership of Man, Woman, & Nature,
by Valerie Andrews

To Honor the Earth

Reflections on Living in Harmony with Nature

Text by Dorothy Maclean

Compiled and Photographed by Kathleen Thormod Carr

With a Foreword by Thomas Berry

HarperSanFrancisco

A Division of HarperCollinsPublishers

Text by Dorothy Maclean

Compiled and Photographed by
Kathleen Thormod Carr

Design Concept by Suzette Curtis and
Kathleen Thormod Carr

Cover Design by Bruce Montgomery

Text Editing by Shoshana Tembeck Alexander

FIRST EDITION

91 92 93 94 95 HCP-HK 10 9 8 7 6 5 4 3 2 1

Quotation on page 109 from *The Outermost House* by Henry Beston. Copyright 1928, 1949, © 1956 by Henry Beston. Copyright © 1977 by Elizabeth C. Beston. Reprinted by permission of Henry Holt and Company, Inc.

Library of Congress Cataloging-in-Publication Data
Maclean, Dorothy.
   To honor the Earth : reflections on living in harmony with nature / text by Dorothy Maclean ; photographs by Kathleen Thormod Carr ; with a foreword by Thomas Berry. —1st ed.
      p. cm.
   ISBN 0-06-250603-X
   1. New Age movement.   2. Nature—Religious aspects.   3. Conduct of life.   4. Animism.   I. Carr, Kathleen Thormod.   II. Title.
   BP605.N48M23 1991
   133—dc20   90-55453
                                                                    CIP

Contents

To Honor the Earth is dedicated in thanksgiving to the Earth itself,
the source of our life, and to all the visible and invisible helpers
with whom we are creating a new Earth.

Acknowledgments

I would first like to acknowledge and thank the Findhorn garden and community in northern Scotland. The seven years I spent there transformed my life and brought me home to a sense of wonder and interconnectedness with nature. This awareness awakened in me the vision of humanity living in harmony with the Earth. It was there that I also met Dorothy Maclean, one of the cofounders of the Findhorn Foundation, whose writings about her communion with nature moved me deeply and changed the focus and purpose of my photography, as evidenced in my work in the book, *The Findhorn Garden*. I am especially grateful to Dorothy for her pioneering contact with the devic realms that is the foundation of *To Honor the Earth*.

I would like to thank the many individuals who helped this book take form over the years. In 1980 Fred Gordon at Findhorn initially encouraged me to feature my photographs in a published collection. I realized then that I wanted to create a book that would complement Dorothy's communications with nature. Dorothy Maclean and Dennis Evenson helped with the initial selection and editing of the deva messages. Suzette Curtis worked with me on the design, and Freya Ziegler and David Spangler helped with the early overall concept. Steven Clark gave valuable assistance in clarifying and writing the proposal. John Button and Peter Koenigs worked with me in the Findhorn Publications Department during the first stages of the book's development. I am very grateful to Clayton Carlson and John Loudon at HarperSanFrancisco for their enthusiastic support when the earliest version of the book was presented to them.

Many others encouraged the book's development by contributing in various ways. Dorothy Fadiman and Phyllis Cole helped to clarify, refine, and further edit the text for another revision, while Trey Scott offered hours of typing.

Donald Keys, Dorothy Fadiman, and Richard St. Barbe Baker (the latter with the help of Michael Soule and Ron Rabin) wrote essays that do not appear in this final version. I would like to acknowledge especially the late St. Barbe Baker, called "The Man of the Trees," who dedicated his life to the Earth, pioneering many reforestation projects in Africa and around the world and helping to save old-growth California redwoods. I am also grateful to Joseph Campbell who, before his death, offered vigorous encouragement during those moments when I had doubts about how the book would be received by the public.

I am deeply grateful to Shoshana Tembeck Alexander for her invaluable assistance in envisioning the final form of this book, her loving and impeccable work in editing the text, feedback on design and photograph selection, and her perseverance as liaison with HarperSanFrancisco in fulfilling my myriad requests. Brad Bunnin and Vivian Greene provided valuable professional advice, and Sypko Andreae and Dave Hoffmann kindly lent technical assistance and Macintosh computers for the final manuscript and design work.

This work could not have been completed without the loving support of my husband Craig Carr, who patiently listened and gave skillful feedback, offered fresh perspective on the text, helped out with the seemingly endless finishing pieces, and cooked dinners when deadlines loomed. Lastly, I want to thank those at HarperSanFrancisco, Mark Salzwedel, my editor who worked to ensure my participation in the final production stages of the book; Michael Toms; and also Jamie Sue Brooks, production design manager, who has been a delight to work with in completing the book's design.

Kathleen Thormod Carr

Foreword

Recently we have begun, once again, to hear the voices of the natural world about us. Not only the mockingbird singing from the topmost branch of the nearest tree, not only the cicada in the evening or the various woodland animals, but also the voices of the sea, the mountains, the rivers. The voices, too, of the winds as these come to us from the various directions.

Some centuries ago we became autistic in relation to the profound communication made to us through all these natural phenomena. We lost the poetry of the Earth under the illusion that the sciences, in describing to us the physical functioning of the natural world, were revealing to us the true reality of things. Poetry and music became not the quintessence of our Earthly experience but something illusory, affected, unreal.

Gratefully, now even scientists are listening more carefully to what they are being told in the observations they are making. They are beginning to appreciate that every equation they write carries more myth and mystery than rational understanding, that science itself is ultimately a mythic mode of knowing.

This is the beginning of our new human intimacy with the larger Earth community. How deprived we have been in these past centuries when we lived within the narrowest intellectual confines that humans have ever experienced! We lost the dream world, the mythic world, the sacred world, the spirit world. Ultimately, we lost the vast world of meaning without which humans become unbearable, even to themselves. The natural world could not function in such conditions. A withering from within as well as extinction from without has been taking place everywhere, for the deeds of humans have an impact not only on the physical forms but also on the inner life principles governing the natural world.

Just as humans cannot endure being ignored by the other members of the human community, so is this also true of the larger Earth community. Intimacy with its human component is vital to the integral functioning and survival of the planet we live on.

Even though we foster ecological and environmental movements throughout the planet, even though we seek to save the rainforests and to renew the regions we have devastated, none of this will ultimately succeed unless it expresses a true intimacy with this larger Earth community. Such intimacy requires an awareness of the unique aspects of each region of the Earth. It requires a consciousness of the many varied species, and of the individuals within each species, as these speak to us from the inner depths of their reality.

Just as the Earth is unique among the planets and each individual is unique, so throughout the entire world every individual manifestation of reality is thoroughly unique. An ancient expression tells us, "The individual is ineffable," beyond all rational understanding. Each oak tree, each willow, every single life form has its own personality, its own voice, its own spirit reality. Each communicates its unique mystery that we never quite comprehend.

How remarkable the creativity of the world about us! Nature never repeats itself, not in the animal or in the plant world; not in the snowflakes or the raindrops; not in its geological structures or in any of its daily displays throughout the observable world. These are all voices of the Earth—spirit voices seeking from us understanding and response.

Our primary response from the human world is admiration—admiration that is also adoration, since each living being presents to us some unique aspect of the divine mystery whence all things emerge into being. How glorious to us the sunrise and sunset, the clouds drifting across the sky! How divine the song of the wood thrush! As Brian Swimme has expressed it, "The universe shivers with wonder in the depths of the human."

In understanding the vast web of interrelations between all natural phenomena—the flow of energy whereby each reality sustains and is sustained by all other realities in the entire world—we come to true wisdom. However, the capacity to comprehend such teachings, communicated to us moment by moment, is a type of literacy long neglected in our society. Yet now we are beginning to understand that literacy in the world of natural forms is of infinitely greater consequence than literacy in the world of human learning.

But the teachings available to us from the natural world are not without paradox. Nature has a violent as well as a benign aspect. There are wind storms, volcanic eruptions, blizzards in winter and drought in summer, floods on the land and tempests at sea. Locust plagues strip the vegetation bare. We might refer to such natural events as the sacrificial dimension of the living world. Within all of them are hidden blessings, attained only by endurance. Only after his struggle with the angel was Jacob blessed.

This teaching is marvelously presented to us here in text and photographs. That the volcanic explosion of Mount Saint Helens could be envisaged as a "balancing dance of many forces and factors" clearly indicates that what is written here is not a simplistic presentation nor some romanticized vision of a purely benign universe. It is rather a realistic interpretation of both the delight and the pathos of the world about us.

We survive at the tolerance of the angel presences that bring us the seasons of the year and the fertility of our fields. We have the capacity to inflict severe damage on natural processes, yet we can seldom do much to restore wholeness. As the title of this book reminds us, beyond all the physical injury we may have inflicted, the greatest damage is the dishonor that we have paid to the Earth. We have been unaware that the community of the Earth is a single community. Reverence will be to every creature, else it will not be at all. The world we live in is an honorable world. To refuse this deepest imperative of our being, to deny honor where honor is due, to withdraw reverence from divine manifestation is to place ourselves on a collision course with the ultimate forces of the universe.

This question of honor must be dealt with before any other question that is before us. We miss both the intrinsic nature and the order of magnitude of the issue if we place our response to the present crisis of our planet on any other basis. It is not ultimately a political or economic or scientific or psychological issue. It is ultimately a question of honor. Only the sense of the violated honor of the Earth and the need to restore this honor can evoke the understanding as well as the energy needed to carry out the renewal of the Earth in any effective manner.

Thomas Berry
Riverdale, New York
January 1990

Introduction

What are the limits of the human spirit? Of the human mind? Though far more restricted by physical limits than we are, earlier cultures of humanity had a vision of human potentiality that in many instances far outstripped our own. For them, the soul of an individual was part of a universal community of life, a community that did not stop at the boundaries of human form or understanding. As part of that community, a human individual had rights and obligations: the obligation to honor the Earth and all upon it through good stewardship, and the right to be empowered by life and to share in the opportunities to flourish and find fulfillment for our human qualities.

In seeking to experience this community, many early cultures, most notably that of the native American Indians, saw no barriers between the human mind and the realms of nature. It was expected that a person could learn, in the depths of his or her spirit, to commune and communicate with the minds of plants and animals. This was so because, however different those minds might be from the human, all minds, all hearts met and were ultimately rooted in the one spirit of the Creator.

In Western culture, our priorities have been to understand and to expand the human community and its welfare. We have done this with considerable success but in the process have lost touch with that larger community of life whose physical reflection we see in the study of ecology. Paradoxically, while enlarging human capabilities on the physical level, we have developed a philosophy of materialism that has narrowed our sense of potential on other levels of our existence.

This wonderful book, *To Honor the Earth,* can remind us of what we have forgotten. Through inspirational text and evocative photographs, it reintroduces us to our own wider potentials. It reaffirms the existence of the community of nature, of which we are a part, a community of mind and spirit as much as of ecology. Also, it shows us that we do have a power of consciousness, of outreach and communion, that can connect us with that community.

Extensive research on extrasensory perception (ESP) is currently being conducted throughout the world. The evidence is overwhelming that the human mind has the capacity to interact with the universe beyond the capabilities of the five senses. At the same time research of a different sort, on the edges of theoretical physics, is revealing to us a universe that is anything but materialistic in the old sense of that word, a universe of interrelationships and connections in which mind or consciousness in the purest sense is the primal "stuff" from which everything else springs. We are moving toward a vision of reality that older generations would have termed mystical, a vision that allows us to reach out in communion to our universe in ways that may seem strange to us but that are familiar and ancient in the history of humankind.

Dorothy Maclean has learned this art of reaching out, of lifting her mind into the place of the one spirit that joins us all. Touching the heart of life's community, she shows us a way to gather insights beyond the realm of human perspective. Her gift is not unique. If we search our memories and our hearts, each of us can remember moments of expanded connection, when it seemed as if all the world were pouring into us and we into it. Such moments can be exhilarating, filling us with a sense of wholeness. They can be frightening, too, for they seem to threaten the narrow boundaries of the self which we have come to accept as the norm. Yet, in imagination, in dreams, in prayer, in contemplation, in wonderment, in the presence of beauty, and in actions that stretch us to our limits, we return to those moments. We flirt with them. We dare them to

touch us once again, fearful that they will but hungry for their gifts of insight, of inspiration, of fullness. Dorothy long ago lost her fear of the transcendent and thus can invite us to do so as well. Her gift of communication with nature may seem wondrous, but it is also very natural and very human.

These transmissions from the devas remind us that we are overly chauvinistic about the meaning of mind and consciousness, which we view, naturally, only in their human terms. We are now coming to see, both through modern science and from a reappreciation of the wisdom of more ancient cultures, that our model of mind is not the only one that can exist. Dorothy's communications with the devas are the touch of a different kind of mind, mediated through her inner gifts into a form generally accessible to all of us. Their power is to awaken us to other perspectives on reality, as well as to our own inner power to contact and share those perspectives.

However, Dorothy's gift offers more than a picture of the psychic and mystical potentials within us. More importantly, it gives voice to a part of life long unheard in our culture. These communications awaken the part of us that knows its communion with a living Earth and, knowing, can empower us with the love that such a communion brings. Not just the source of the messages, but also their content, is vital. It is the gift of an invitation to join with our world in a new act of wholeness, so that as the limits fall from our spirits and our minds, we may find new companions to explore the richness of creation.

David Spangler
Issaquah, Washington
November 1989

Preface

Nowadays the effects of human impact on the environment is front page news as we begin to see clearly that what we do to nature, we do to ourselves. We are discovering that we are part of nature and it is part of us, that we are inextricably bound together. Our physical connection is obvious, but are there spiritual links as well? Most cultures on Earth have given credence to beings of nature—nature gods, nature spirits, elves, fairies, and the like. But starting with the industrial revolution, our Western culture has turned its focus to the physical world, designated nonphysical beings as creations of the imagination, and declared humans to be the sole bearers of intelligence.

I, too, lived with the assumption that only human life is intelligent and capable of love—until one day in meditation the still small voice within asked me to harmonize with the essence of nature. As this inner knowing had guided me safely and wisely for the previous ten years, I was willing to try this assignment even though I had no idea what it could mean. At the time I was living with a small group of people in northern Scotland, and we were just beginning to grow a vegetable garden. Unknown to us, these small beginnings would one day result in the renowned Findhorn garden and community. At the time, however, all our concerns were immediate and practical.

I decided to try contacting the essence of the garden pea, with astonishing success. Then the following day I contacted a presence that was linked with the land around us and that could also answer our questions. For want of a better name, I called this the Landscape Angel. From that point on, I daily tuned in to the essence of various plants and received answers to our questions on all aspects of tending the garden, from watering and fertilizing to planting and pruning. Over time, as these communications revealed more about their source, I perceived the deep wisdom inherent in the essence of nature.

I began to understand that these "beings" I was communicating with were actually the manifestations of an intelligent forcefield that had been interpreted in different ways by different cultures through the ages. They told me that they hold the archetypal plan and pattern for all forms and aspects of creation, and that they fulfill their part in the divine plan by wielding the energy needed for the growth and development of form. I called them angels or devas, the Sanskrit term for angel, meaning "shining one." Though using the word *angel* for the intelligence of nature, I perceived I was communicating with an energy field that had no static or human form. The biologist Rupert Sheldrake's term *morphogenetic fields* seems to refer to the same energy. It was the conscious and intelligent essence of each plant species, a group soul, that I was contacting.

There is a part of each of us that is of the same essence as the devas. We might call that the soul level, or the spirit. Thus any of us can "listen to" and "talk" with the angelic world, because we share the same worlds within us. Love and appreciation are the bridges between us.

In my experience, the inner essence of all nature's forms is wonderfully loving but not emotional. When I visited a grove of redwoods that were being saved in perpetuity and saw that they were dying, I wept in anguish and turned to the Angel of the Redwoods. It consoled me with its perspective and its peace, saying that even if the trees toppled, their vibrations were forever part of its contribution to the planet. This noble view from eternity, rather than reconciling me with the death of these trees, instead strengthened my determination that the majestic redwoods be saved for the world. The angel was certainly not condoning the felling of the trees, but I believe the tree intelligence understood that our human emotions are spurs for action. I think the quotations in this book made the need for our action abundantly clear, and it is the role of those who have made the blunders to find the solutions. It is our role to tap and organize the power of our wholeness and, with love and without condemnation, to take action on behalf of all life on Earth.

Since that first contact with the Pea Deva in 1962, my appreciation for the angelic world, this unseen yet basic side of nature, has deepened, along with a greater awe of the wonder and beauty of nature. They have connected me with the outer world, helping me to realize that the ability of the North American Indians to listen and to watch the processes of nature is the basis of their intimacy with the land. I have become more conscious of intelligence not only in nature but in all aspects of life as I have met angels of sound, color, healing, peace, air, fire, machines, animals, cities, countries, the planet.

In this book we are focusing primarily on the perceptions I have had from the aspects of nature connected with the plant world and the elements. There have been animal contacts too. For example, the cetaceans proved fascinating. When I attuned to the overlighting soul of the orca, I was aware of a complex brain, which was very difficult for me to understand as it functioned in a way different from the human. Of course, it did not have our cultural assumptions! The orca intelligence seemed to have a greater sensory awareness of its surroundings than we do. It also seemed forgiving of ways humans have mistreated orcas in the past. Urging us to relax and have fun, it affirmed, "In love we can play together, and any errors in our past relationship would be dissolved. We do not cling to the past; the present is what is now. You need not feel guilty, not with love."

The angels not only taught me the value of linking with nature but also continually reminded me of the truth of our own essence. They see with a perspective beyond our limited time and space and thus see the great potential we have as humans. They see us as creative beings who will lift up all life when we walk the Earth in love. They see us learning to consider the whole in our actions and interacting with them to recreate the Earth. When we stop blindly reacting and learn to act in love in all situations, this will happen. Individual growth on the part of each of us is needed.

Ultimately, the message of the angels is about the oneness of all life. They say that humankind can learn this truth and come to live in harmony with the universe. They invite us to work in cooperation with them, offering to help in ways we have not yet imagined. They acknowledge and support our role as creative beings, and they never cease to believe that we can learn to initiate ways that resonate with the whole.

What nature says to us awakens something deep in our hearts. The angels speak in joy, of joy and eternal things, even in the midst of their concern for how humanity is affecting their work on Earth. They remind us of our destiny as builders, not destroyers, of the whole of the planet. They urge us to a greater unfolding. Their message is one to listen to, embrace and act on.

This book presents some of nature's viewpoints, translated, of course, through the terminology and understanding I brought to my communication with the angelic realms. The text is excerpted from contacts made over a period of twenty-five years. Most quotations are from the years 1968 to 1973; this is simply because during that time I was learning by attuning to nature how interwoven we humans are with all planetary life, and I was translating into my own words the insights perceived. Now that I am more deeply grounded in inner attunement, I have not felt the need to record my perceptions in writing.

Through her photographs, Kathleen Thormod Carr brings another perspective. For her, photography is a way to explore the essence and inner radiance of all life and to communicate those feelings. Our association over many years has culminated in this presentation, which offers a greater insight into the wonders of nature than either of our ways alone. May this book help you to discover your own attunement to the divine within and without.

Dorothy Maclean
Issaquah, Washington
January 1990

We bring breaths of open spaces and hills, of sunshine, showers, and breezes. All of these are part of your being. Even if you live in the midst of a busy city, these natural things are home to you. They are part of the atmosphere of this Earth, part of the surroundings in which you live and grow. Even if your life and thinking are completely enmeshed in the human world, still you are part of our deva world, which works for the perfect flowering of all life. This is your birthright. You may turn your back on it, but someday you will learn this truth and live in connection with all life on this planet. Only then will you tap your highest potential.

Gentian Deva

Chapter 1

The Wisdom of the Angels

My contact with the angels of nature taught me a new way of seeing. Like most people, I was used to seeing and thinking only in terms of outer form. But they taught me that all life forms have inner patterns or forcefields. For example, we can "see" the inner pattern of a magnet from the way it arranges iron filings around it, or the crystalline structures of water in the patterns of snowflakes. These are the inner forcefields made visible. All of these forcefields are continually in movement and are susceptible to being influenced by the power of human thought and feeling, for we humans, according to the angels, are the creative power on Earth.

They suggested that I learn to think in terms of inner forces by looking at all forms as made of light, glowing and radiant. In this way, I could acknowledge the inner patterns. Besides thinking of plants as light,

I also practiced imagining my own body as light. To my surprise, my body did seem to become more vital and dynamic, even lighter in weight!

As builders of form on the planet, the nature angels have vast wisdom. However, this wisdom is not of the intellect; it is rather pure primeval intelligence, a deep knowing that is completely integrated into the whole. I loved the experience of being at one with this loving intelligence. It was hard, though, to put their perspective into words, simply because our language is geared to dealing with concrete and distinct outer forms and not with their boundless dimensions. Nevertheless, I tried to translate as accurately as I could the subtle levels of perception they were sharing with me.

For instance, the Apple Deva described, using the poetic and perhaps accurate metaphors of sound and light, how various forms come into existence. I found the explanation of the process fascinating and had to expand my normal ways of thinking to understand how the subtle vibrations of the seed idea passed into increasingly slower vibrational levels until they culminated in the fully manifest plant. In various ways, they taught me to expand my conceptions about the miracle of life.

Joy is a pervasive quality in these inner worlds of nature. That may seem strange at this time when nature is being threatened on all sides, with many species of life becoming extinct due to human encroachment, misunderstanding, and greed. But I found that the nature of life itself is joyful, that deep within the core of each one of us is the joy that indeed surpasses understanding. This is a joy beyond polarity—a joy that includes sorrow, a hope that embraces despair. The angels' perspective comes from the vastness of infinity and beyond time; from there, they radiate love to everything without judgment. In silence, we too can contact that center. Nature asks us to do that and to find our unity with all life. As if my brain had to have this concept engraved on its cells, the angels stressed the interconnectedness of all life again and again.

However wise and powerful these angelic envoys from the inner formative realms are, they insist that we humans have the same wisdom and power within us—and beyond that, we have the gift of being the creative force on this planet. To me their main theme was not how to grow gardens or how to understand life but the injunction to attune to the uniqueness of our souls and accept and act on the powerful love in our core. 🙢

As from the seed a tree grows, so from a seed idea a pattern of force issues forth into creation, passed on by silent ranks of angels. At first the idea is still too unformed and unfixed to endure any but the most exacting and silent care. Growing in strength and size, the pattern becomes brighter until, still in the care of the outermost great angel, eventually it scintillates and sounds, its forcefield steady and brilliant.

Then the pattern is passed on to the makers of form, the elements. They give of themselves to clothe that pattern. This is a continuous process: the pattern is apparent everywhere in the ethers, held by the angels and made manifest beyond time. Then, at the appropriate opportunity, through the ministrations of the elementals, it appears in time and place, in the beauty of the blossom and the succulence of the fruit.

This is the word made flesh. This is how all creation is held in balance by great layers of life of which your conscious mind is unaware. A miracle? You need a greater word. You need to go beyond words.

Apple Deva

We see life in terms of the inner force. You see only the outer form without recognizing the continual process taking place. We would like you to try to think in our terms, because it will make things easier for both of us. You will be closer to reality and will also be able to understand us better.

Inner forces are as intricate as outer forms, having shape, color, texture, and so on but of a finer and richer substance. When you look at plants, know that what you see has an inner counterpart simply pulsating with life. When you think of the plants as glowing and moving with life, you in fact add to that life. At the same time, it puts you in touch with the Source of all life and generates more power and more life all around you.

Landscape Angel

Do you truly appreciate the wonder of a plant? On the inner levels where energy is particularly clear and powerful, we hold the pattern in consciousness. On the outer levels, these different energy patterns appear: each leaf distinct and beautiful, each flower exquisitely planned and executed, each seed carrying its own life message. Each plant has a flavor, scent, and power of its own. Some plants heal a wound, some help the eyesight, some balance emotions. You are each intimately related to plants and to all creation on Earth and beyond. This is the miracle of the oneness of life.

Life is delicately adjusted for its fullest expression on this and other planets, and the whole is affected when a part is out of balance. Millions and millions of years have been needed to bring the vehicles of life to their present state of sensitive interrelationship. Now that lack of human sensitivity is threatening this life, it is essential that you be more sensitive, that you appreciate the miracle of life—the ever-present glories and marvels around you, the vast and purposeful concentration of energies making possible the privilege of Earth life.

As you expand in consciousness through your wonder and love, so will you expand the planet into its greater destiny.

Rue Deva

$\mathcal{F}$eel into the intensity that we are. The purity of it awes you. If you feel deeply enough into anything, the purity is awesome, for you approach the center of life. We are glad that we can momentarily help you sense the stillness innate in all life. That stillness is the central part of our being. Without this sustaining core of quietude, the vibrations that appear as color, scent, and shape could not issue forth. This is the natural order and rhythm of life, something for humans to regain. You live on the surface, avoiding your inner core, and so you lose your way. Surely every flower shouts to you that the way is to live in tune with the inner solitude and from there to radiate out the perfection of creation.

Aubrieta Deva

All is sound, all is vibration. We, the Angels of Sound, are not limited in form by what you hear through the ears. We sound a note, as on a trumpet, and the sound goes forth all around, like the circular waves from a stone thrown in a pond. The note is diffused throughout the atmosphere. We sound it and sound it until the whole atmosphere vibrates with it. The note does not grow louder but rather more intense, so penetrating that it permeates everything around, like mist permeating the air, influencing everything in its presence.

We know the individual notes for all in our charge, and we sound them, like tuning forks, to be picked up by each plant. When a seed is ready to germinate, moisture and warmth do not of themselves set its note vibrating; we do that. We set the seed on its way and hold out its note before it to follow.

Listen to the sounds of nature. They are so diverse that it is difficult to hear all at the same time. Even if a note is harsh, it is not discordant, because it arises from the spirit of each creature and thus has no sound of self or separation in it.

Angels of Sound

When we ask you to think of plants, or anything, in terms of living light, we are not trying to detract from the beauty of the world as seen through human eyes. We want to add to that beauty by making it even closer to the reality. By thinking in terms of light, you add light to that already existing.

Humans drastically change the face of the Earth, thinking only that you are shifting matter when you level ground and vegetation or extract minerals and oil. If you think of everything as living light, as vital substance, you will alter the landscape more thoughtfully. But alter you must, for your thinking is creative.

Think in terms of light and all creation will respond. All creation is light, even if obscured by human misperception. Consciousness unfolds as humanity links outwardly and inwardly with higher octaves of life. Love the light and change the world.

Landscape Angel

*W*hy should humanity act as if it were the only intelligence? All around, the angelic world is bursting with awareness, full of knowledge and truth that would be of inestimable value to humanity.

The same one life flows in our veins also. The more we all recognize and act on this, the more will all worlds come together in unison. In truth, we are all children of the one creation, all part of one life, all here because we are meant to be here. You could be dynamos of power and transformation, but you have limited yourselves, and in limitation you can do dreadful things. Why not open out to all of life?

Deva of the Golden Conifer

What fun life is! For us, to hold each little atom in its pattern is to hold it in joy. We see you humans at times glumly encountering experience, doing things because they have to be done. We marvel that your sparkling life could be so filtered down and disguised. Life is abundant joy. Each little bite of a caterpillar into a leaf is done with more zest than we sometimes feel in you humans. We would love to shake the sluggishness out of you and have you see life as bright and blooming, waxing and waning, eternal and one.

Mock Orange Deva

Nothing is worth doing unless it is done with joy; in any action, motives other than love and joy spoil the results. Could you imagine a flower growing as a duty and then sweetening the hearts of its beholders?

Devas of the Fruit Trees

*T*une into nature until you feel the love flow. That feeling is your arrow into the angelic world. Always it is your state of being that the nature world responds to—not what you say, not what you do, but what you are.

The Devas

Chapter 2

The Power of the Elements

In ancient times, Western sages considered all creation to be composed of four elements: fire, air, water and earth. To them these four elements were symbolic of various qualities. Fire, for instance, was a metaphor for dynamic creativity. In our everyday language, we still accept that image and talk of "the creative fire," of "burning away the dross," of "the fire of love." Air represented communication, human interaction, the idea of flying, and we talk about "the breath of inspiration," and "airing" one's opinions. Water was symbolic of movement and of the emotions, of sensitivity; we say that time "flows like a river" and talk of "getting into deep water." Earth stood for practicality and stability, so today we ask "what earthly use" some idea or gadget might have, commend someone who is "solid as a rock," and acknowledge that an "earth-shattering experience" shakes the "ground of our being."

Indeed there is much truth in the ancient view. In fact, we could liken the elements to basic components of the universe as expressed in modern science: energy, space, time, and matter. In essence, fire is analogous to energy, air to space, water to time, and earth to matter.

On the physical level, we speak of the "power of the elements" but often forget about this power until a hurricane batters our coasts or an earthquake devastates a country or a river floods a major city. Then newspaper headlines shout about disaster. The angels showed me another perspective, helping me realize how short-sighted, and generally condemning, we humans are in our interpretation of events. The fury of the elements usually redresses some imbalance or initiates a new order, and it also takes the human factor into account. For example, my curiosity led me to attune to Mount Saint Helens when it first began rumbling. There I encountered an intricate, exacting, balancing dance in which many forces and factors, including the human, were being delicately and benignly considered by the overlighting angel in order to attain the best results for all concerned. The angel talks about "the explosive tendencies of fire, especially at these volatile, changing times," referring not only to the volcanic fires of the mountain but also to the human creative mind and its technology, which is changing the planet so rapidly nowadays.

The angelic oversoul is always connected to the form under its auspices, even when that form is found beyond our own solar system. This I discovered when I noticed a particularly beautiful stone on the moors by the Moray Firth in Scotland and decided to attune to it. I expected a very simple, unevolved presence, because we humans have put the mineral world into our lowest category of life. Instead, to my amazement, I found myself at one with an enormous spirit that stretched out into infinity. I called it the Cosmic Angel of Stone, and it reminded me that we are indeed linked to the stars.

The angels continually harp on the theme of oneness, the interconnectedness, of all life. Modern science says something similar in equating matter and energy. We humans are evolved enough to be consciously aware of that oneness. For many of us that connectedness is best felt in nature. Watching a sunset, walking in the rain, spending a quiet time gazing into a fire, working in a garden, even simply taking a breath—all of these are opportunities to realize our inner links with all of life and the elements that compose it. ❧

𝒴ou are children of the elements, composed of and part of the elements. The world and your bodies were made so that you may find and express the joy of all creation, but you are destroying yourselves because you think you are separate from the rest of life. How can you possibly think you are separate? How can you not know that when the wind blows, it is part of you? The sun gives to you and is part of you with each sunbeam. From the water you came, and the water joins you all. Without the air you breathe, you could not live. How can you not know that if one suffers, the whole consciousness of the Earth partakes of that? And when one rejoices, the whole takes part.

Love all of life and become one with it. All of life is part of you.

The Elements

FIRE

*T*he Angels of Fire wield the fire of the sun. What an immense role they have to play! Nothing can live or grow without warmth, yet nothing can destroy like fire. Across millions of miles of space, we can still feel this power. And that is only a portion of the substance of fire. Apart from what we have discovered and measured already there exist even more potent energy levels we have not yet touched. These are not only a food for life but a generator of life itself. The beings who manipulate these forces carry on a fingertip something more explosive than an atom bomb, but they control this power and use it sensitively for the whole.

Meditation

We are aware that adjustments must be made that have an impact on the whole. Volcanic mountains are always linked with and aware of the larger network of connected forces beneath the surface of the Earth. These in turn are affected by what happens above the surface of the Earth. Though we do not make the calculations and decisions about earth changes, we are aligned with them, one in intention, a vehicle for plans and decisions that are part of the whole. Given the explosive tendencies of fire, this is a delicate task, especially during these times when humanity has aggravated the volatile tendencies on the planet. Our ingenuity is needed to blend all forces to a fine, polished result.

Volcanoes seem powerfully uncompassionate to you humans, but this is not so. The strength of the fire element is needed everywhere: in your bodies, in your smelters, in the earth, in the suns. Recognize that power in yourselves and dedicate it to the whole, and also be accurately precise in the gift that power gives.

Angel of Mount Saint Helens

*L*earn from the energy of fire. We destroy, we consume, we transform, and in the process we bring health and warmth to life. You are in an era of change when old ways are breaking down. Accept and move with that change in yourselves. Let acquisitiveness or greed or desire for power burn out in you. In their place will arise a clear field of awareness of the whole. Love and sharing will grow in you, as will the creative fire to find the means of expressing them. Fire melts and tempers; let the fire of love do the same with you.

Spirit of Fire

AIR

We praise the Creator with air. We stretch from world to world and around each one. We give to life and are life. In each world we are different, perfect for each one, making a gift of ourselves for you and for everything alive. We hold sound in our hands, we promote change, we make tangible to you the warmth of the sun. When you breathe air in, you breathe in the essence of the Creator. You can attune to us by recognizing the One in whom you live and move and have your being. We unite you all in the One.

Devas of the Air

*L*isten to the breeze. This sound of nature is a mantra, a note that holds life in it. If its vehicles, the silent trees, are removed or overlaid with human sounds, a firm footing has been lost. What does this mean? The sound of the breeze imparts to us a certain spiritual quality that balances some of our other qualities. Without it, some of our worst aspects are accentuated.

Sound is creative. As physical life evolved, the sounds of the forests became helpful in nurturing humankind. They continue to be helpful, indeed essential, for the health and balance of the physical body.

Meditation

You do not know which level is most characteristic of our essence: the soft zephyr, the rollicking gale, the raging cyclone, or something beyond all these. Come deeper, below thought, as in the still center of a cyclone, and imagine our evolution on this Earth. As with your bodies, we are the result of millions of years of evolving patterns. Imagine the effect of an atomic bomb on our volatile media after aeons of ordered advancement.

Yet we are intimate with humans, to whom we bring the breath of life from the Creator. Breathe in that breath in absolute quiet and realize the oneness of life. It is so on the physical level where you depend upon what the Earth produces for breath and food and clothing, and it is so on the higher levels where we are finer, more intelligent expressions of life. Nothing is static, most particularly in our realm of air. Do not try to pin us down, but let us try to understand one another.

Spirit of the Wind

WATER

*E*ach lake has its own quality of uniqueness and its different influences, even as does each rainfall. Humans are one aspect of those influences. But when you focus on the human element, you can forget that meanwhile life is flowing on. So many parts make up the whole; life is so fluid. What is there to grasp hold of? The flow, of course, which is a torrent in your heart. Then you too can let the love flow to whatever may come. It will stream over and incorporate all obstacles—even rent increases! Love and economics are not of two different and mutually exclusive worlds. Swim in the flow of love and all worlds are compatible.

Angel of Lake Ontario

$\mathcal{F}$eel into the returning rain as it hastens back to the earth. Are not all components of life inextricably linked, one with the other—the water longing to descend and the vegetation longing for it to come? And when their oneness is accomplished, does not the soft, green harmony of growth spread over the land, all creation rejoicing in it? Everywhere you look, everywhere you listen, the same story of the interrelationship of life is told. Beyond your senses, in the inner worlds that cause these effects, the same refrain repeats itself in endless variety.

Landscape Angel

Rain has passed through many influences. It has been lifted from the land by the great drawing power of the sun, and it falls again with the natural currents of life. Rain is not just hydrogen and oxygen; it has many intangibles that cannot be measured, qualities lacking in your treated water. The natural processes have a magnetism that you cannot imitate.

You can cooperate, however. When you water plants, you can radiate intangible qualities that are as helpful to the plants as the natural ones that come with the rain. When you act as part of the one life and love all life, you are a transformer for many ranges of vibrations.

Landscape Angel

EARTH

$\mathcal{W}$hat is earth but the very substance of this planet, refined through aeons of time? It is the seedbed of life, free and available for all life. That immense purity you sense in the devic realms applies to the earth itself. You say, "Cleanliness is next to godliness," and you wash the "dirt" off your hands while at the same time polluting the earth with that which annuls life. Yet that dirt, that soil, is itself sacred, and it is humanity who is degrading it. Let us both fulfill our functions through the cleanliness and liveliness of earth.

Landscape Angel

Mountains are the strength of the Earth itself. We maintain the world by continually translating forces up and down, our pores always breathing. We are older than time. Whatever the weather, we spread its energy out into the surround, out from the depths of the earth, and out from the heavens. We are pure rock, with our heads in the mist, arms in the loch, and feet deep inside the earth. What we do is too timeless for the human mind to grasp. It has no beginning and no end. However hard we may seem, our work is purely beneficent. Such softness comes out of hardness worn down.

Spirit of the Mountains

*T*he life force in the soil comes through the soil population. The transforming of matter or minerals into a form capable of a higher vibrational level—the process you call evolution—begins at the most basic level. The soil population plays a vital part in this. A plant pattern comes into existence by using soil, water, heat, and air. All these are drawn into form by the invisible workers in the elements. These you call the soil population on one level, fairies on another level. The necessary elements in soil are materialized through fungi; that is why fairies and toadstools are connected in myth. These elements can also be materialized through the power of focused human thought. According to how strongly you hold the pattern in your thoughts, the process can be speeded up and made manifest, almost out of time and space. This is what cooperation between humans and the angelic realms can bring about.

Landscape Angel

*T*hough you have contacted me through a tiny pebble, I am concerned with vastly more than your planet, for I am connected with the mineral life that exists in various stages through creation. Nature is full of paradox; you seek contact with what you consider a lowly form of life and, in fact, contact a universal presence. The human mind codifies and formulates, which is within its right and purpose, but you forget that all is one, that God is in all, and that even the most basic substance of life, which seems devoid of sensitive consciousness, is held in existence by its opposite, a vast consciousness extending beyond your imagination.

It was the beauty of this particular stone that drew you to me. Consciousness of beauty brings you into oneness with any part of the universe. The more you appreciate beauty, the more you are linked universally. The glory of God is everywhere, stretching from the farthest reaches of the universe to the little grain of sand, one and the same thing, held in eternal love and timeless with life.

Reverence all life. Emulate my patience. Unfold the mysteries of God, even of pebbles. Be a learner of life, a revealer. Let your dominion be over yourself, and let your expanding consciousness see God's life in all things.

Cosmic Angel of Stone

Chapter 3

The Call of the Trees

From among the hundreds of messages I have received from the soul level of the mineral, plant, and animal worlds, only one species, the trees, has called urgently and powerfully. The angelic intelligence of the trees cried out for action on the part of humanity. From the perspective of the angelic world, it is vital that we change our views on the value and the importance of trees, the skin of the Earth, where vital change is needed. Time has certainly given authority to the urgency they expressed. The destruction of forests—tropical, rain, and temperate—all over the world is now endangering the life of the planet itself.

We have long known of some of the services trees render the planet, such as holding the soil together, balancing water tables, absorbing carbon dioxide, providing homes for many species. We now realize more precisely, as years ago we did not, some of the ramifications of these services. Tree felling is the cause of many so-called natural disasters, such as floods and droughts. Destroying trees, the respiratory organs of the planet, contributes to the greenhouse effect. We know that the rain forests harbor a vast selection of plant

genes, which can be used in many ways to help humanity, especially medically. Yet trees are at this time still being slashed, burned, and felled at the rate of two acres per second.

Even on mental and emotional levels, trees have a major influence. The nature of their being brings steadiness, peace, and countless lessons on the inter-connectedness of life. They have their own aura, their own sound and scent. All these things affect us, and the lack of them disturbs our balance and can impede the development of our higher sensitivities. Probably all of us recall the experience of leaning against a tree and gradually feeling calmness enter our being, or coming into a forest and feeling awed, humbled, and quieted by the great trees. Tree intelligences once suggested to me that large cities would benefit tremendously by having substantial areas of trees adjoining them that offer refuge and peace from urban sights, sounds, and smells, which would help stressed city dwellers return to sanity. City parks do help in this respect, but they are "sanitized" and thus do not extend the powerful freedom of more natural woodlands.

Despite the negative impact our actions have on trees and their functioning, the spirit with which they respond to us in these messages is vast and noble. They say they see us rather like teenagers learning from our mistakes how to behave and grow. Always they acknowledge and encourage our magnificent potential as human beings.

The devas urge us to act, to use the power that is ours as humans to bring the planet into better balance. Acting on information regarding the need for trees entails vast changes in our viewpoints and in the organization of society, both economically and socially. The trees see the power of the human will and imagination to go beyond our fears and change outmoded systems. No doubt they perceive that, in any case, our short-sighted policies in forest management will have to come to an end sooner or later, when we have cut our last virgin tree. We will then be facing the economic dilemma we are now trying to avoid. But *now* is the time to change and search for alternatives.

Most of all, the trees see that we can use our great power in the thought and feeling worlds. By this I mean aligning all parts of ourselves—our physical bodies, emotions, minds and souls—so that intuition guides our actions. This is what human development is all about: recognizing that we are part of nature and committing all of ourselves to that greater whole of which we are a part.

When we "listen" within and without, we find that we are one with the universe. Perhaps trees are the aspect of nature most conducive to learning that truth. They shade us, shelter us, and become the flesh and bones of our homes. Throughout our long past we have had a close relationship with trees; in the present they can help us relate to our true selves. Let us ensure them a future. As the Czech theologian Comenius wrote in 1632, "As far as possible, men are to be taught to become wise not only by books but by the heavens, the earth, the oaks and beeches." The trees are calling us to our greatest potential, for the sake of all life. ❧

G reat forests must flourish. Humanity must see to this if it wishes to continue to live on this planet. Your need for trees must become as much a part of your consciousness as your need for water. We are the skin of the Earth. Skin not only covers and protects but also passes through it the forces of life. Nothing could be more vital to the life of the planet than trees.

Leylands Cypress Deva

*L*arge trees are conductors of energy. They stand ever ready, channeling the universal forces that surround and are part of this planet. They are carriers of especially potent vibrations, sentinels of cosmic energy, transforming the power in an aura of peace.

Large trees are essential for the well-being of the Earth. No other can do the job they do. They and humanity each represent the apex of a particular form of life, and you can gain much by association with them. It is no accident that the Buddha is said to have found enlightenment under a tree.

Let your love go forth to the trees. Give thanks for their creation.

Landscape Angel

$\mathcal{Y}$ou can render the greatest of services by recognizing the greater life of trees and bringing our reality to human consciousness. We, the overlighting intelligence of each species, are what is behind the growing self-awareness that is life. Just as humanity can function in various dimensions, so can we. Nature is not a blind force; it has inner vehicles just as humans do.

We do exist. You who are coming to wholeness will recognize us with your higher minds, in spite of your intellects, and then God's purposes for us both will be fostered.

Tree Devas

Many lives come and go, and still our power goes up to the sky and down to the earth. Our serene strength stabilizes and makes upright whatever comes to us, for we are living matter, fashioned from the elements, and we are kin to all life. You and I are blood brothers and sisters, made from the same substance, fulfilling our individual destinies on this planet. I contain you in my towering strength, and you contain me in your towering aspiration. We are tree and human—and we are much more. We are representatives of divinity, and we never end through endless ages.

Humans are despoiling our power on Earth, interfering with our destiny, but in the process you are learning of your own destiny. We hope that one day you may proudly take it on and enrich the Earth as never before. You can indeed do so with your enlightened love.

Cedar of Lebanon Deva

*C*hildren of Earth and Spirit, we address the spirit aspect of your nature, for there is our meeting place. We are not in harmony with the part of humankind that rapes the land. Nowhere is that rift more pronounced than when ancient trees are thoughtlessly felled.

We repeat, tall trees are needed. It is not enough to have the land reforested, for young trees are not capable of fulfilling our task of transmuting energies. You need mature trees for that. If there is a dearth of large trees, the peace and stability of humans is affected, for we are interconnected. You need us for the balance of peace and stability. You cannot destroy us without destroying yourselves.

Tree Devas

*W*e of the plant world have our pattern and destiny, which we have fulfilled throughout the ages. But now because of human encroachment, we are not allowed to be. We have our portions of the plan to fulfill; we have been nurtured for this very reason. But now many of us can only dream of the spaces where we might fulfill ourselves. The pattern is ever before us, out of reach, a dream we are forever growing toward but seldom attaining.

Monterey Cypress Deva

Come closer. Rest in our strength. Become aware of the smaller notes that we play—the flutter of leaves, the shining glints of color, the sunshiny softness of spring. All are connected with the birds, the insects, the elements. A large tree is a place of beauty, a family, a home, a country to explore. A refuge to many, it stands proud, giving out to all, reaching up to the sky and deep into the earth, enduring. The tall tree stands as a symbol of a particular perfection of God. Let it stand, and you will come closer to God.

Copper Beech Deva

Chapter 4

The Promise of Cooperation

Cooperating with nature is an idea we in the West do not normally accept, because we have assumed that we are in command of nature and it is ours to use as we desire. Besides, how could we possibly cooperate with a nature we also assume has no intelligence?

However, on the level of essence, nature does have intelligence, and we, with the same essence within us, can resonate with it. When we do, our thoughts and feelings have great power in the subtle realms. The angels suggest that this cooperation can take place in ways yet unthought of and that as we act in love and respect toward nature, many secrets will be unveiled. They have also told me that cooperation can even offer solutions to major problems such as pollution. When we live in an attitude of love and peace, our power and nature's purposes can be linked as never before.

We have, of course, long influenced and altered nature by creating plant hybrids or new animal breeds. But when we learn to cooperate with love, without force, the results will be even better. Luther Burbank made no secret of the fact that he used love in his highly successful plant experimentation and development. All life responds to love, and we ourselves can find the balance between apparently harming a plant by cutting it and enhancing its vitality through our love. I have seen a supposedly mutilated bonsai plant radiant with life. And when we start to use our technology in a loving manner, we can transform what has often been rape of the Earth into change beneficial for all.

However, some basic natural patterns are to be respected and not altered. When I attuned to the Brown Bear Oversoul—which almost cried with joy because it was not used to love being focused on it—it reminded me that animals cannot step out of their pattern in the way we fluid humans can. Therefore, when coming across a bear in the wilderness, it is appropriate for us to remember its bearness and know its habits. Such respect is a form of love. The Black Bear encouraged us "to walk in love," saying it knows when we do and that such an attitude helps all creation. The Grass Deva, also delighted to be in touch in consciousness, said it was glad to be producing food for many, and the grass was glad to be walked on by appreciative walkers who recognize its awareness.

Yet sometimes we have to deal with a form of life that we might consider a pest. What do we do then?

Some people consistently get results when they ask animals, plants, or insects to cooperate. I, however, had a most painful time when first learning to cooperate with moles in the garden. I was afraid my requests of them would not be followed, so I first contacted them with a lot of doubt. It was not until after several years, when I saw evidence of the mole taking a route I had suggested, that I turned into a believer. We all have freedom of choice and must act on what seems best to us. With freedom comes responsibility, and if we seem forced to kill an ant, for example, after using commonsensical and nonpoisonous means to keep ants from entering our homes, we must consciously accept that responsibility. Again, attitude is most important.

No matter how much specific information we might acquire regarding the natural world—and using our intellects is essential in life—the attitude with which we use that information is primary. We are ignorant of much of life, and we have much to learn. For instance, once after our group at Findhorn in the early days bulldozed an area of gorse and grass to make way for a building, I knew something was wrong and consulted the Landscape Angel. It reminded us of our lack of consideration for other life in the soil, our lack of love when using machinery, our lack of apologizing for the mess. As always, new horizons were revealed.

Human cooperation with the forces of nature, wherever it has occurred, has yielded wonderful results and taught us to relate to the planet more realistically. Although the vitality of nature in wild places is far greater than that in urban areas, the possibility is open for the same power to be present in cultivated areas. I have experienced such a garden in suburban Holland and knew that the gardeners there loved and respected plants in a spirit of cooperation.

It is impossible to give rules about how to cooperate with nature, because each of us has his or her own unique way to follow, which can only be discovered individually. Love and appreciation are always our surest links with all life. In our human process of unfolding ourselves, we enter into cooperation with both our own inner capabilities and the archetypes of nature itself. ❧

*U*nless you become conscious of the divine within yourselves and act from that, you are open to grave limitation. To be in touch with the true nature of life, you must be conscious of our existence. We play such a great part in the formation of your world, but until you recognize us, there is no true cooperation. Recognition forms the bond on which to build.

Landscape Angel

We rejoice at human cooperation. We have always been willing to do so and rejoice now because you are reaching out to us. The initiative must come from your side; we do not force ourselves on you. We have always been part of life on Earth and of human endeavors, even when you have been unaware of it.

We can cooperate in many ways you have not considered. While all the energy we wield works according to pattern and law, with human help and creativity it can be used in a different form. For example, we can help humanity minimize pollution as you strengthen our energies with your conscious love.

Landscape Angel and Devas

*I*n the past we have taken what we could get from the planet and thoughtlessly used in a few years what has taken millions of years to produce. That is a passing phase in our history, for when we take on our stewardship of the planet, joined with all beings in love, the deva world can impart some of its secrets, knowing they will be used for the good of the whole. Then a world can be built in scintillating joy, for limitless energy is available—the same energy that produces universes.

Meditation

Whether it rains or the sun shines, whether the wind blows or all is peace, the controlling consciousness behind the outer forms is undisturbed. As you too remain calm and centered in any storm, you link up with and control all worlds. Our patterns, as expressed in the plant world, come through in perfection because they issue forth from a still center. Your purposes too can come through in perfection as you hold clearly to them, undeterred by outer events. This is law; this is the creative power given to you and to us to wield. There is chaos in the human world because every wind of chance is likely to blow you off course from your purpose. When you do hold fast to purpose, you are creative masters of the world, our brothers and sisters, ready to meet the changes that are part of life.

Southernwood Deva

Human influence has upset many branches of life. As all life is interconnected, such interference is bound to reflect on you sooner or later. But we can work with human desire for change. As you offer yourselves and call on our power, we can use our joint power in directions not otherwise open to us in your world. In fact, this is a way of cooperating that would lead to strong results. Conscious cooperation is always more potent.

Landscape Angel

Humankind has dominion over the Earth and has arranged and planted gardens within the limits of the material world—often very admirably. But when you grow gardens without awareness of the divine life as expressed through our kingdoms, you cut yourselves off from a large part of life. That is why untouched wild places have a magic and vitality lacking in even the most beautiful cultivated garden. However barren the wild places, there we can be in fullness, without the constrictions of human consciousness. There we can be free. And there too humanity can find healing.

Horse Chestnut Deva

*T*he plant patterns are held in our world, and each detail of them is carried out to perfection. Why then, you wonder, do freak growths occur? Life is never static; there is always openness to change, a moving onward of life. All creation has an element of experimentation, or else it would stagnate.

Often in the past there has been a great sense of cooperation between a gardener and ourselves in producing some lovely new variety. That sense of cooperation has largely vanished as humanity has manipulated the plant world for its own selfish purposes.

You get better results from a child if you use love, not force. Although force may bring quicker results, it starts a chain reaction of effects. The same is true for us. You have used force on nature, resulting in imbalance. There is another way to produce change and new varieties of plants, and we hope that you will cooperate with us in it.

Foxglove Deva

Regarding bulldozing: It is important to consider the dwellers in the ground. Seek to ameliorate with your love the harsh workings of the machine. Apologize for any harm done, even though it may not be your fault. You cannot wash your hands of any action done by anyone, for you are all part of it, but you can add your energy to the situation in a positive way.

Landscape Angel

$\mathcal{W}$e who control the storm spirits seem wild at the moment. The weather has indeed been influenced by humans. For example, you have desecrated the land by your mining operations and slag heaps, taking without giving. Likewise, you use the atmosphere around the Earth without proper consideration. Thus you upset the balance and clear a pathway for destructive winds.

The powers in our control are subject to natural laws. When humans interfere and break these laws, there must be consequences. But perfected human thought can perform miracles, and we would wish for that.

Angels of the Air

On a rainy day you can appreciate the good in the weather and act in a way that is appropriate to it. Always look for and find the unique flavor of each moment and each place you find yourself in, not wishing for something different. You would be amazed if you could see what a difference this makes to the life forces. Each moment has its own beauty, but it can be nullified if you resist the flow and put yourself out of harmony with it. To go with the natural rhythms is far more important than you realize. Inspiration comes on all levels when you are relaxed in the flow of life.

Landscape Angel

*T*ake care not to fall into depression and negativity, particularly when it seems so strong in the world. It is that which makes our work difficult; the opposite uplifts humankind. If you wonder what you can do about the problems of the world, know that you can help by affirming and living out the basic decencies in your own life. By basic, we mean that divinity at the core of humans. That is your polestar around which all revolves and to which all evolves. With that you move with universal force.

Spirit of Canada

God is love. As creation becomes more conscious, it expresses greater love. The essence of life, no matter what its level of consciousness, is love. Life becomes more perfectly itself when surrounded by love. This is true of all realms of being. Humanity's greatest contribution to life on the planet is to love consciously and so to bring more health, vigor, and beauty to life.

Landscape Angel

I remind you that any action, however small, taken on behalf of the whole makes a tremendous contribution. Never consider yourselves powerless. Never consider that the situation is hopeless. In this time of great change you are the catalysts of change, part of me in our ongoing, our unfolding, our purity. Together we are a blessing.

The Planetary Being

Notes

Notes on the Photographs

*All photographs were taken with Nikon cameras using 24mm,
55mm, and 105mm lenses, mostly on Kodachrome 64 film. The
only filter used was a polarizing filter.*

Biographies

KATHLEEN THORMOD CARR

Dorothy Maclean

was born and raised in Guelph, Ontario, Canada. After graduating from the University of Western Ontario, she worked with British intelligence during World War II. Later, while living in Britain, her search for the essential qualities of life brought her into conscious communion with the divine within. In 1962 she joined Peter and Eileen Caddy in founding the Findhorn Community in northern Scotland. There her attunement with nature helped produce the famous Findhorn garden.

In 1973 Ms. Maclean left Scotland for California where she cofounded the Lorian Association. She now divides her time between Washington state and Canada and conducts workshops with Ron Rabin called "Bonding with Earth—Aligning Personal Vision with the Unfolding Intention of Spirit." Her work with nature has been described in *The Findhorn Garden.* She tells her own story in *To Hear the Angels Sing,* and collections of her meditations have been published at Findhorn as *The Living Silence* and *Wisdoms.* She has published a booklet, *The Soul of Canada,* and is currently working on another book.

For information on talks and workshops, contact: ConTerra Associates, 280 S.W. Clark St. C-1, Issaquah, Washington 98027.

SHOSHANA TEMBECK ALEXANDER

Kathleen Thormod Carr

is a freelance and fine art photographer. She was born in 1946 and received her B.F.A. (*cum laude*) in photography from Ohio University in 1970. She went on to study with Minor White in his home in Arlington, Massachusetts, and was strongly influenced by his sense of presence and metaphor in photography. This quality deepened in her work during her many years as a photographer at the Findhorn Foundation in Scotland and at the Esalen Institute in Big Sur, California.

Kathleen has traveled and photographed extensively in Europe, North America, and South America. Her work has been published in numerous books and periodicals, including *Esquire, New Age Journal, New Realities,* and *Cosmpolitan.* She was the main photographer and photographic editor for *The Findhorn Garden, Faces of Findhorn,* and *The Findhorn Family Cookbook.* Ms. Carr's photography has been exhibited and sold both nationally and internationally. Her companies, Carr Classics in Big Sur, and Earthlight Nature Images (2126 Green Hill Rd., Sebastopol, CA 95472), produce fine photography greeting cards, T-shirts, and other photographic products dedicated to honoring the Earth.

Ms. Carr lives in Sebastopol, California, with her husband Craig and their two cats.

Touch the earth, love the earth, honour the earth, her plains, her valleys, her hills, and her seas; rest your spirit in her solitary places. For the gifts of life are the earth's and they are given to all. . . .

—Henry Beston